Bless This Home

poems by

Alison Woods

Finishing Line Press
Georgetown, Kentucky

Bless This Home

ACKNOWLEDGEMENTS

Thank you to Steve Addabbo, L. S. Asekoff, Jean-Marie Christman, Alfred Corn, Jennifer Franklin, Diana Goetsch, Jack Grapes, Alexandra Lehmann, Marion LoGuidice, Luisa Maisel, Molly Peacock, and Samantha Woods for your gifts, and your particular insights into various stages of my writing process.

To my mother, for her encouragement and support. To my daughter, for being such an incredible human. She inspired this book into being.

Jordan Tamagni, from the beginning, and ever-present. Sally Lipton Derringer, for her tireless championship and encouragement, her balanced and keen eye!

Thank you to the Catwalk Art Residency, Catskill, NY, and the Virginia Center for the Creative Arts, for the time, support, and space to write. Also, sincere appreciation goes to the editors of the following publications and journals, in which some of these poems first appeared (sometimes, in somewhat different forms): *BigCityLit*, "Tether," *Connecticut River Review*, "Canary," *Poetry East*, "Ice Dancer," *Rattapallax*, "Pandora's Box," *Rattle*, "Lena and the Flying Cranes," *Salamander*, "American Folk Art," *The Paris Review*, "Hirschfeld's Ninas," *The Westchester Review*, "When You Can't Expand Anymore and Not Fall Off."

"God's House" appears as lyrics on the CD titled *God's House* by Marion LoGuidice.

Thank you to Chuck Connelly for his generosity, brilliance, and permission to use his painting for the cover of this book.

Publisher: Leah Maines
Editor: Christen Kincaid
Cover Art: Chuck Connelly
Cover Design: Howard Grossman

Order online: www.finishinglinepress.com
also available on amazon.com

Author inquiries and mail orders:
Finishing Line Press
P. O. Box 1626
Georgetown, Kentucky 40324
U. S. A.

Table of Contents

iii.

For my daughter, Lavinia Woods

In memory of Kate Light, and Martin Mitchell

i.

Magic Show

We're here in the gilded theater, elbow to elbow,
close as we are able to conjure
given the velvet seat divider.

Uncertainty prompts our gasps, then applause;
the magician releases himself from the many knots
he has bound himself to.

A small box tapped twice and we reason out the dove
who appears from beneath the bellowing scarf.
The light-tricked halo clings tight

to a magic bred this deep: the sleights
of hand, the rabbit's foot,
the girl he saws in two.

This House

Vieques, Puerto Rico

Through the wide bars
of the jalousie

the sleek peninsulas
of horse's muzzles.

Others have found
their way here, too.

We wake to find them
shifting their weight,

looking down upon us,
gleam of the silver moon

on their backs. *Give up,*
they say, *on permanence,*

memories of childhood,
and quiet despair.

They've come to witness
our awakening,

and lean gently
into this house.

Johnson's Pond, VT

A summer porch party
moves to the edge of a field,
a hive of bodies, a bonfire,
pond-cold ale. Some are

stripping now, clothes fall
to the ground. A dark-eyed
boy sways his ass in a slow
striptease, they're howling,

and you, distant observer,
long to rewrite this, shed
your clothes and while you're at it,
the meaning of hesitation,

you who comb your hair
thinking of God as the hot sun
relaxes your bones. Slip off your sundress.
Stand naked as Eve, modesty offset

by the serpent circling your ankle.
The sly snake says *stay*.
The sinners watch from a distance.
You enter the pond.

Tilt-a-Whirl

In '92 it was a kind of freedom to knock-about,
straddled on the back of his motorcycle, Lake Charles

the smallest city I had ever lived in. Walking beneath
looming Cyprus trees, all I felt was an eagerness

to feel, boudin spilling out of its casing caused a stir.
It was a dream. We met in the library, soon married.

Then made a daughter more mine than sunshine.
His papaw called me Sassafras. That first night

we found a carnival by the lake, a wink from the man
who opened the gate, our tickets fluttering down.

The thud of beanbags missing their mark beat
in the background while the chemical plant's sunset

blazed more brilliant than the original and we sat,
knee to knee, pressed into the deep seat of the ride.

Southern Cross

We wake in a trailer, corrugated tin braced against dawn.
Nothing will insulate us from the hard future, not calico-
papered walls, not cinnamon-scented candles.

He leaves for the refinery in Nomex coveralls,
silence broken by dogs rattling their chains out back.
Gravel shifts beneath tires, sun spools through leafy trees.

Like a sailor navigating his future, he rose to the top
of iron crossbeams as dawn finished its fiery show,
the Southern Cross a shadow falling across the work boots

of men down below. He was witness to the budding stages
of heaven, miles of steel organs blowing off steam, and the rain-turtles
men drew in the dirt to egg on summer showers, an early whistle.

Men twice his age bragging about the women who almost caught them,
the ones who fill their thermoses. I loved that trailer's rickety rooms,
sneaking sex while his mother made us coffee, light and sweet.

Deer Season

Calvin's home—his mustard yellow truck
pulls up, dips into several abrasions
in the road along the way,

rattle of dishes on a knick-knack shelf.
Taut face, tobacco skin, he carries work
shirts from the cleaners, *Calvin's Auto*

oval patches on the pocket. There's a buck
tied to the roof of his pick-up. I am engaged
to his stepson who does not hunt, but instead

hides his poetry, so not to be teased, a sheaf
of papers under the bed. For a while we all live
together, plus his mother, beneath a mohair sky

where juniper spills along the cow fence,
and the air smells mossy. Here, amongst ammo
and gumbo, between long pillars of cypress,

our predicament: each of us a hunter,
hungry, and also marked, grazing
in the crosshairs, prey.

Pandora's Box

The most powerful cameras can see the past
and record it: a star that lived and died
giving light, as when we touch someone
so deeply we become permanent,
even when we are no longer together.

Two people meet for dinner on Broadway,
the entire breadth of their past in the way
they approach their meal; the ravenous
and the dainty get what they deserve
and then decide how to feel about it.

This is how our lives shape us, a physical
incarnation of our souls' mishaps and naïveté.
It is good and simple and perfectly natural
to be afraid of what keeps its distance from you.

In the Museum of Natural History

Diorama, headdress, colorful ceremony.
Everything stilled in fate.
Daughter, you moved inside of me.

I was almost a mother and already
dutiful (walking, as the doctor instructed,
to induce labor). The halls

are mammoth: kayaks behind glass.
Cherokee women stared back at me.
Soon you will ask: why has my father

abandoned me? Navajos praise *Grey Bird
Drinking From A Ditch, Elk Prancing*. The Cree
prepare for winter, a prayer for rain and wheat and yet

to name you means you belong to me.
Women turn seed to bread, a task of faith.
Iroquois came into the world from mud

on the back of a grandmother turtle. A ripe moon
unloads her passengers into the fields
of mother-love, my *Wren in Snow*, my *Bright Papoose*.

Canary

Coming home, I found a lost bird.
His owner had taped fliers to lampposts,
& in thick black marker: a phone number.

Who's going to find a canary, and return him
I thought, until I found myself climbing
the hood of a car, cooing, trying to save him

from the wilderness of the city. I was a new
mother, working for a mortgage company,
climbing out of the subway most days focused

on the exact next right step, and here I was,
holding this canary, feathers
exploding in my hands.

Schooling

My daughter dreams
there are fish on her pillow,

she stands over me,
looming in the dark.

My daughter finds me
alone, no one else

beside me here, the empty
place host to the bias of us.

I let her in and the dream
expands, shoal of us

fitful as bonefish
fining in the shallows.

I've grown used to her
swift entrances, shadowy

disturbances that bid
and accumulate, algae

on a conch, and I know
we're in it for the long haul,

for the knock and spill,
for whatever casts

into our net as we drift
among the flying fish.

Tether

Sometimes I forget I am a mother.
The earth in turning night to day
illuminates our home, my life, its cover,

turns my eye away from hovering
over my child's eager display.
Sometimes I forget I am a mother,

looking to love's other
possibility, and that is okay
to illuminate my home, my life, its cover.

Sometimes fearful of regret's deep shudder—
life being judged by those who stay—
I sometimes forget I am a mother,

yet being one, we are each other's lover
reveling in our own play
that illuminates our home, my life, its cover.

Then it dawns. She is my tether,
my next right step, my right of way.
Sometimes to forget I am a mother
illuminates my home, my life, its cover.

The Eclipse of Our Selves on a Fall Afternoon

I was not meant to follow the phantom all the way to my door but here I am, inviting her in. When the day grows this quiet, I know something precious lies in shadow. My daughter goes into her crib at 1pm, a gleam in her eye. She knows all of language yet refuses speech. Instead, she tassels my hair askew. Sometimes she tires of me, but she tries not to let on. I repay her, I let her meander through the crunchy leaves, I Iet her hug every tree. This morning, if I could choose, I would say *happy*. As if love were a simple thing, dignity, threads of sun in her hair.

Daughter's Tattoo

Against my permission she got a tattoo.
Now a tiny black moon and star rises
with her left hand and sets when she is idle.

Next a bear with wings, a sword for her love
of Medieval literature, a shield for Kurt's
record label, a bone for our dog, a heart

writ large, open and empty, and to my surprise,
my initials carved into her forearm. She's art's
tableau seeking ink, Higgins Black Magic

soaked into her bloodstream, pain, permanence—
she's exuberant as she meanders through
the dark forest of self-rule.

Baxter Land Preserve, North Salem, NY

My daughter woke heartbroken this morning,
shivering in a well of tears. We share
a season of heartbreak, two generations,

two females, plus our dog who barks
at a lone stud grazing. The dog tries to get
his attention, the equivalent of love

in any denomination, canine, equine, or human.
Dog and horse square off: tresses, snout, hoof, paw,
his glorious mane, her visible quivering,

one yelping, each with a calling. The horse
swats a fly, blinks a dark-honed eye
while our dog briefly disappears.

What else do we have if not the freedom
to turn away and leap into a tangle of holly?

ii.

Between Heaven and Sparta

The nurses have found us here, safe
as Zeus was when they placed him in a cradle
to hang from the branches of a tree.

There is always something approaching,
even as we have just arrived, a pile of shoes
at the door. It is dark. I could write of loss

but suddenly there is only accumulation,
a light snow tumbling. Always something
belonging to a river rushing away.

Late September, frost on the cornucopia.
The nurses brush our foreheads with pink,
waxy lips. Love, we are nestled in the crook

of God's bent arm. It is a boomerang,
he'll send us sailing.

Dig

Into the plaster of this prewar building's wall
the way a feather might bring down
a house of cards
time and pressure
just beginning to form

we are looking for our parents
in the next room which means
it is the seventies, nothing but density
a leak
in the beanbag

so we dig
a hole
in the wall
with a spoon

we scrape like mice
mining plaster
which dislodges
in little clumps
& planes of dust.

Dark Forest

Oh mama,
you are sleeping
all the time. I pull
the dark around me
like it is a friend of mine,
and all I see is your body
lost in lakes of air,
I reach for you there.

Oh mama,
what am I to do?
Your hand is heavy,
heavy as a shoe, amber bottles
filled with pills lie on their side
like little submarines.

Oh mama,
your bedroom's dark,
dark as a cave, as if
no light has ever shone,
and I adjust every day
to shades of sadness
that fill the air,
these closed circles
that we share.

Oh mama, I'm lost
in lakes of air.
I take you in my arms
and am lost in the damp
dark of your hair.

He Believed

My father sought acupuncture
on Canal Street in the seventies,
sought relief above fruit stands and ducks
on rotisseries. His spine, not a spool, not mine,
not a pillar, not fine. Scar tissue, he said,
as if torn inside. He'd take the IRT downtown,
stop for a feast of roasted meat with crispy skin,

then his skin needled with a stainless tip.
I imagined steep stairs to treatment rooms
stocked with ginseng, powders, herbal perfumes.
He believed pins twisted clockwise might redirect
the pain that settled in. How it grows in this world
of wild sensation, nestles between muscle and bone,
especially for father, who traveled alone.

Hirschfeld's Ninas

are about connection: his daughter's name
woven into a plume of smoke.
While my father drank coffee, and smoked,
I learned to find love hidden in the scrawl.

Woven into a plume of smoke,
I'd sit on the bed with Hirschfeld's illustration
and learn to find love hidden in the scrawl,
while my father watched football.

I'd sit on the bed with Hirschfeld's illustration
seeing, layer by layer, how to untangle it.
While my father watched football,
I examined the cursive script

discovering, layer by layer, how to untangle
what amounts to thousands of tiny dots.
I'd follow the cursive script,
his daughter's name sewn into clouds.

What amounts to thousands of tiny dots,
a constellation in black ink.
His daughter's name sewn into clouds,
tucked safely into the buckle of a shoe.

Her name embroiled in the nub of a scarf,
a constellation in black ink.
How to find love hidden in the scrawl
and layer by layer, untangle it.

God's House

I went to God's house pregnant
and whispered in his ear,
for the love of mercy help me,
but God did not appear.

At seven I became a human being
when I realized I was asking
God to take away my pain,
and found that I was praying.

I went to God's house to sing
and chanted loud and clear,
and thought about the times I'd asked
for help from my despair.

I even put God's picture
in my father's breast pocket;
as he lay in the pine wood coffin,
I cried on the sea-green carpet.

I've pronounced the ancient language
word-for-word, and held him in my heart.
I've felt release, and tried to be
devoted, human, and a part.

What innocence I have is splendor;
I am corrupt to the bone. I go to God's house
to remember from where I come from,
and I sing to keep on remembering.

Tumbleweed

The planet offers earth,
and loam, but sometimes
soil refuses
moisture, then
love travels
like tumbleweed.

Remember when father moved out
and mother was not leaving
bed or fog no matter
how much
the future
was waving.

Whatever has happened,
or was supposed to,
it rambles down the road
of what once was.
It is a dream now,
almost bearable.

Goodbye to the willow.
Goodbye to the ransomed heart.
This path of thorn and mint
goes on and on, sprig
and poisonous berry,
with which I write my name.

American Folk Art

The Wife of a Man Who Was Lynched

She is staring off to the side,
her face dark, round as persimmon.

On the scrap-metal lawn
dusk is about to break.
She takes in the laundry
hanging now, stiff as birds.

An American flag is flapping
in crisp hard folds,
the threadbare cloth,
the blank white stars...

You can see the pasture's
gone gray with grief.
The woman fending
for life in the gathering

dusk, unpinning
the winged white sheets,
feathering, feathering in her hands.

In the Hospital Again

i.
Not a crease
on the bed sheet,
only the slow sound
of his breath

collection of bones
too light
as if he might
fly away.

ii.
Relieved for the thin
sheet that covers
what is missing
my eyes slip

to the concave
starched white depression
where his leg
once was.

iii.
Passing through
the corridor
to the street—
father, father

I am breathless,
or so full of breath
it seems I am breathing
for the two of us

air has entered my chest,
is streaming up my throat,
knocked clean in the vacant *oh*
of my mouth.

iv.
Outside, the clock-shape
of Columbus Circle
swathed in dusk, scaffold's
crazy pitch breaks light

into pieces, and you—
four blocks away, perhaps
you have already forgotten
the route home

as you lean toward
that one band of sun
on issued sheets.

Ice Dancer

She swims a universe of air and whirls,
the opal eye, a storm of grace unfurls,

and with it she becomes unknown, or new,
balanced on the sharp edge of her shoe.

With force of breath she drives both will and weight
into the leather strapping of her skate,

and plows her body past an invisible barrier,
and quietly moans, crackling like fire.

Descending in pirouette she sees her image
laid out upon on the ice, it pays her homage.

The echo of her thoughts sounding a terror
as she defaces the disquieted muse in the mirror.

Tracing hairline patterns in the immaculate sheet,
at the height of furor she is complete.

She finds in form a beauty she creates,
a shield against the world, which she obliterates.

Through skill and mastery of teeth and blade,
there comes a moment she is not afraid.

Model Boat

We knelt beside the stone lip
and set our boat onto the water,
its white sail, blue pinstripe markings
that made it our boat, my father's and mine,
our faces floating along with the trees,
lapis, already a few fallen leaves.

He was telling me something
about love, and then to seal it,
when he was sure I had it, he said,
"let her go," and I released her,
heading out toward the center,
suddenly lost among the other boats.

iii.

One Fish, Two Fish, on Lex

I am thrust open, shucked oysters
served upon the polished amber
of the bar. In this life I have
staved hunger with bread and butter,
but you offer Blue Points, they flower
on ice between us, bearded sea creatures
in their seat of loam and blue pearl.

I am what the ocean left behind,
briny concoction of lust and sentiment.
Like Venus, I love the rough waves wracking,
the frayed net where all erodes except
the deepest part of me, and I remove
seaweed scraps piece by piece, still eager
to taste a bit of salt.

Moonshine

Hooch, white lightning
distilled in the hickories.
Moonraker, I have loved you
by the still, loved you by the sea

from grain to starch, fucking
or lovemaking, I was a junkie.
From out yonder I hear
some people need care,

prone to the broken down
sugar you once were to me.
Your essence is outlaw;
the clandestine way you convert

mash to whiskey. Love
is lawless, far as I can see.

The Shape of Stars a Paradox of Reaching

Remember the stars'
resilience, how you
repeated my name

like a song. It was
the start of something
we can never

catch up to.
The evening you
poured water

from a bucket,
my daughter
a baby

in the bath,
trying to catch
the thin stream

that slips through.
It was impossible
to not notice when

she ran from the tub,
stars shooting
from her eyes.

Later, I heard you
repeat my name
like water through

cupped hands, you asked,
what do we do now?
If I promise

to heal you, forgive me
my lie. Cover me
with your smoky

presence. Dull me
like a scar in the dusk-
riddled sky.

When You Can't Expand Anymore and Not Fall Off

We did not live beneath one roof, did not share a sink or soap
or payments to the electric company. We barely ever woke together,
yet this love consumed me like no other. He was ether, filigree,
a night cat in a fable whispering riddles in the alley.
It was like when something retreats, leaving the mark
of its existence, how you comb the long shadow.

Empty Church

We stood inside where the light was dim
compared to outside where we had been
killing time. A dusty piano in the corner
by the pulpit. He played an original song
he'd been writing for decades, unpacking
a deep baritone. The church was nowhere,
a shadow to the somewhere I belong.
He took my hand, began to propose, then
laughed as he shut the piano's eyelid,
closed its heavy door. Whether truth or lie,
it doesn't matter anymore.

As Night Repeats Itself, So Do I

These riots of thought—
God's skin dark against
this house, shuttered,
a plateau of sky.

To be empty of you, near
monotone, a canary
yellow lamp glows
even as the eventual

approaches. Loss,
ancient as moth's breath,
its feathery beat
against the linen shade.

From The Naturalist's Handbook I

I've been longing to untangle
the fly from the trap, and all the injustice
found inside botany and flora.

The day loiters in an alternate reality.
Birds lift, dart as I approach, and I wonder
how the naturalists ever get close enough

to tag talons. And now, with him gone,
disappointment is no longer
a thing that comes through word or deed,

it is more like a species that exists,
a flowering plant with stinging hairs,
sharp nettles. In a way we are

the undergrowth we trample upon.
Once uttered, words are like flies in traps.

From The Naturalist's Handbook II

The chicks have cracked through their shell, zygote
conceived in a cluster of confusion: fidgety,
chaos of new light.

Who will protect them? How long must I stay
drop-feeding, fluffing hay, tending
to their tedious incubation? These chicks

are my future, egg, yolk, meringue.
My body's heavy with its yearning and refusing.
States of embryo need a fierce hovering.

Frothy, hawk-like, their wingspans widen.
Over their entire yellow, mythic beaks
peck at the thin membrane. Wizards

of phenomenon, they work all night,
until they accomplish their freedom.

On Being Ordinary

Unrealistic to think we stand out any more than the golden flash
        of some small fish making its way
in a life concentrated by blue
        and the undependable sun. There is the desire to find one place
that is not water, beyond this tangle of seaweed
        and broken shell. Tasseled by unseen currents,
our bodies are preserved in salt like this. Lather peaks,
        and copper sheen melts along the surface
as if even the sun gives way to something.
        One day, white sand covers his one fish-eye,
without ceremony. The sun steps out of its blue-green sock,
        basking in its own brilliant reflection.

Rushing Water

There's got to be another word for rushing water,
and if there happen to be two people watching,
one for the casual witness, and one for the other.

There's got to be a word for the throat of the flower
where pistil and stamen join. Or the way a diamond
feels in the hands of a miner as it is lifted from earth's

crusty socket. There's got to be a word for clergy bathing
in the same stream, the onomatopoeia for what has died
in the wet bevy of molecules, silver and blue.

There's got to be a word for water rushing over a fallen tree,
how long it took to get here, and more rushing water to follow,
there's got to be a word for this.

Dandelion

It is spring,
the planet opens
its corset,
dandelion cotton
everywhere
around earth's
dark bones
of containment.

All winter
I was plowing
bitter fields, my soul
an orange poppy
about to crumble
like burnt newspaper.

Now I scatter
bags of black mulch,
I garden, I walk the dog,
I admire the path
I've made between two
boxwoods, a lilac,
and a blue star juniper.

Healing will never
make me whole again.
Some days, all I have
is this onslaught
of noticing their delicate
stems and fine mop-top,
a white fuzz halo.

I exhale
my deepest wish,
the seeds scatter,
dandelion spores
adrift.

Apples

It is the last batch of apples for the season
so it should not surprise you when they bruise
and turn mealy. The mealy apples are not beautiful.
We shared a season, a moment. What is beautiful
is the way we try to harness feelings into a lifetime,
how we succumb to our hunger. The fierce
living we do because we have to, the inordinate
power we put into the hearth, while here.

Ever After

Across the rippling of the pond in Central Park
a model boat floats in its own oily shadow,
tilled white wing skimming the water.

Oh this voyage! A lifetime
to ask what love is, the good
questions a fragrance filling the air.

I know there are moments
mired and unreachable,
but then some pleasure, like dawn,

slips out from behind the curtain.

Metamorphosis

If I am to enter the family Nymphalidae it should take
about two weeks. I already envision flying, and that
is a good thing. I was captive, knocked from every angle.
Now I have black margins, a tawny orange overcoat, and wings
that beat as nectar eases into my throat. I am finally resolved
to float. I understand what it means to emerge from a chrysalis,
to mimic the Monarch, to wander in a flight pattern of gold.

Lena and the Flying Cranes

after the Moscow Circus

The duo are high-wire walkers,
a swing-act thrilling audiences, acrobats.

The stakes could not be higher
as the accordion of her body unfolds.

She leans out over the cusp, steps off
into the violent husbandry of gravity,

her body folds like origami, inward, fetal,
a triple somersault, then elongates into a fluid

concentration of muscle. The way she travels
through the air, the brushstrokes of her body

an aura of light. She is all language, with swift
punctuations: as she flies, she defies all we fear

to be true. Homing, with precision, she inhabits
abandon, the intense vulnerability of creation,

smoke and ascending violins as she reaches for
her catcher's hand, the human grasp pulling her back

onto the ledge, and the beginning of boundaries,
a retreat from the overreaching darkness.

Fire Island Ferry, End of a Season

I'm on the ferry heading back, trying
to be finished with this unending quest;
love and sex, bow and stern, the wake
that parts and splashes in our forward sway.

Move on, he said, as if yesterday
I wasn't queen of his social calendar,
student of his geography lesson, map-keeper
to our secret cache of sky.

Anything not bolted down I release
for the sake of buoyancy, what scatters
vexes only me, not the salt air, not the sea.

Port and starboard, like arms, embrace
many lives making the transition from water
to land, leaving one paradise for the other.

Alison Woods was born and raised in New York City. She studied creative writing in the graduate department of McNeese State University, Lake Charles, Louisiana, poetry at Brooklyn College in New York, and earned a Master of Fine Arts degree from Columbia University in New York City (1996), where she was awarded a Division Fellowship from the School of the Arts. She has studied with such notable authors as Allen Ginsberg, Robert Olen Butler, Lucie Brock-Broido, Lucille Clifton, Alfred Corn, Daniel Halpren, Richard Howard, and Alice Quinn. Her poems have been published widely in literary journals, and her chapbook, *Dark Forest*, won the New Women's Voices Chapbook Competition from Finishing Line Press. She has collaborated with singer-songwriters including Steve Addabbo for his CD, *Out Of Nothing*, and Marion LoGuidice on her CD *God's House*. Woods has taught poetry in the New York City Public Schools and in a variety of workshop settings. She currently lives in Dobbs Ferry, New York.

CPSIA information can be obtained
at www.ICGtesting.com
Printed in the USA
FSHW010040071020
74473FS